Contents

Some words are shown in bold, **like this**.
You can find them in the glossary on page 23.

What is yellow?

Yellow is a colour.

What different colours can you see in this picture?

The colour yellow is all around.

Have you seen these yellow things?

What foods are yellow?

Bananas are yellow.

You peel the yellow **skin** to eat the banana inside.

Some cheese is yellow.

It is made from milk.

What yellow clothes can I wear?

This raincoat is yellow.

A raincoat will keep you dry in the rain.

These yellow boots are made of **rubber**.

They keep feet dry in the rain.

What is yellow at home?

This toy duck is yellow.

It is made of **plastic**.

This towel is yellow.

After a bath, it is good for getting you dry.

What is yellow on the road?

This sign on the road is yellow.

It shows that a fire station is near by.

This yellow rubbish truck is
on the road.

It takes away the rubbish.

What is yellow in the park?

There are yellow flowers in the park.

They have lots of yellow **petals**.

There is a yellow slide in the park.

The park is a good place to play.

What yellow things are on a farm?

There are yellow chicks on a farm.

Chicks are baby chickens.

Some animals are fed yellow **hay** on a farm.

What yellow things are at the seaside?

This umbrella is yellow.

It protects people from the sun.

People can wear yellow flippers at the seaside.

Flippers help people to swim.

How do people use yellow at work?

People can use yellow trucks
to move dirt around.

Some people wear yellow **helmets** at work.

Helmets help keep people safe.

Quiz

What yellow things can you see?

Look for the answers on page 24.

Glossary

hay
dried grass for feeding animals

helmets
strong coverings worn to protect the head

petals
coloured outer parts of flowers

plastic
a strong, light material that can be made into different shapes

rubber
a strong, stretchy material used for making things like boots and shoes

skin
outer layer of a fruit or vegetable

Index

Answers to the quiz on page 22

T-shirt   cushion

ribbon

jumper

Notes to parents and teachers

Reading non-fiction texts for information is an important part of a child's literacy development. Readers can be encouraged to ask simple questions and then use the text to find the answers. Each chapter in this book begins with a question. Read the questions together. Look at the pictures. Talk about what the answer might be. Then read the text to find out if your predictions were correct. To develop readers' enquiry skills, encourage them to think of other questions they might ask about the topic. Discuss where you could find the answers. Assist children in using the contents page, picture glossary and index to practise research skills and new vocabulary.